The
I pr.E.lude I

Poetry Blog: www.amazulugaming.com
Instagram: Onepoeticgamer
Twitch: www.twitch.tv/onepoeticgamer

ISBN

Published by
AmaZulu Gaming, LLC

Cover, Logo and Illustrations done by
Christopher James Rowland

Final Edition
Printed in the United States of America

Table of Contents

He/R - The Prelude

Preface

Many moons ago across light and dark, we decided to part to learn what it was to love each other unconditionally throughout time. Through various lifetimes we have found each other and will continue to do so until we ascend back to our eternal place in the cosmos. Before they can be "we" again, HE must find himself before finding SHE. Know that I love you now, then and forever.

He/R -
The Prelude

Souls Don't Wait to Say I Love You

I believe I poetically love you
and I was going to take the time to explain
but thought,
if she doesn't read between the lines
like how she did when she met me
then explaining my love poetically
wouldn't even make sense.

Universal Love

Warm smiles from
I love you whispers in my mind
recognizing signs
quick reminds that find my attention,
taking the time to listen
not in quantitative measures
unless, in fact, you need that
for time itself is spent appropriately
when it's with you
let's pick a few M&M's
(moments and memories)
that are worth the amount of tears and laughs
placed in them,
and as we partake in this feast
the least of my worries are realized
because it's you
yes you,
not the body and skin
but the energy within
where do I begin
with what can't be explained with words,
at least not completely
evidently, we're celebrating the recognition
oneness - sameness - uniqueness
the reunion of a union
from kickstarts that caused contusions
to egos that we let go
to let love flow
from warm smiles.

Dance to the Music

She asked if I made music
and didn't realize
we were doing just that
frequency flowing on digital waves
as we played
on grounds found in timelines
created by our souls,
I suppose my dream enacting behavior
of Wushu lead me to you
right to left,
and what's left is for me
or "we"
is up to intuition
listen, forgive me if my "feels"
come off as predominant,
I'm a giver of energy
of which we all need
but I rather share than take
and what it is
what we now make
is music,
even if you don't think you can
as, from what sounds we now create
I beautifully watch you
dance.

Nature of the Song

When you speak
I hear currents of water flowing
nourishing molecules that
make up my existence
I placed you on my wish list
so that when I dream
I need not a genie
to manifest your presence
find we dance in rhythms
like katas
sounds made in air pockets
with more than just hands
out of body experiences
that place this journey
beside the Universe itself
in too deep in shallow depths
depending on perception
butterfly connections
with wings that turn snakes
into dragons,
if you hear laughter
it's from moon lit belly music
where wolves howl in spirit form
to find direction
at first I thought I was guessing
until I noticed that
your soul winked at me first
birth this idea from the conception
of meditation and prayer

I no longer have to wonder
as since entering synchronization
I heard exactly what you are saying
from currents made through water
by your soul.

Feel My Vibration

Eyes reflect lights of green
she has to see
healings in hue
of my being,
be only you
as none other
can be on our frequency
be it dialed in
plugged up
in synch,
this is the only way we know
to combine our souls into
what we use to be
before choosing to find each other
in this dimension.

Frequencies

The sweetest blue
came through 12 AM convos
where I listened to you breathe
Cleo Soul giving off harmony
that places me in frequencies
at 528 Hz
dialed through Time to
see your Face
if this kiss has to be made through pixels
it's just as pleasant as what I imagined
been waiting for this all day
bypassed the things I'm supposed to do
cause all I can think about
is you,
can't escape
in my mind you've replaced
sub-conscious attempts
to focus,
love on my lips and fingertips
that should appear as blips
in territories uncharted
like what's between hips
sipping super moon reflected lights
like water acquired from Fiji springs
it feels so good
to feel nature
like soft grass under my feet,
you are a mixture of the Universe
presented as a gift to my eye

in 5D vision
the sweetest blue
oh yes
the sweetest blue.

Searching for He/r

When nobody looked for me
no one cared to be
I head you singing heavenly
saying,
you wanted me to stick around for good
I should but there I stood
cause I could-not hear you
be who, you knew
but it's cause I didn't C through
the right I
when I let my, third eye
bye-to-try
as this is do or die
another lifetime where this guy
doesn't learn this lesson to get next to your essence
would be purgatory
the allegory of the story
is I can't ignore the
vibes sent between stars
across the Universe
into this verse
watch me sue pur
whoops let's reverse
pursue U through my super
power, clock the hour
sunflower shows it's 11 minutes past 11
and I'm sitting on a cloud next to heaven
thinking how to manifest this next blessing
here's to us, let's pass this test

and, when nobody looked for me
no one cared to be
I heard you singing heavenly
saying…

Jen

Look Jen
generally I don't do this
gotta move gently
cause there's something else to it
who knew dis would generate a genesis
of emotions I pursue with
ill flows, here goes
generously spit verbs, moving feelings
genetically, but only for you I do this
took the red pill for direct truth
poof, genuine gentleman
giving you gentians
add it up, hand and hand
let's exchange oxygen
over blends, chi tea, feeling grand
and, I'm not nobility
poetic gentry making memories
through melodies, poetically
genetically made to touch your soul
heavenly, cause presently
I'm gifting this spoken word to you Miss Lee
generating a flame to you from me
from B, powered off ginseng
wake up to hear you sing
tasty like ginger snaps, hopefully this brings
gentrified changes, move winter type feelings
into the generable passion of spring
hope this could be more than a one-time fling
and I have to throw the pitch to see if you swing
so look Jen, I hope you see what I mean
gingerly writing these thoughts to you, I'm sending.

Munch Over Brunch
(Shoot the Shot During Lunch)

How do I
get her to notice, get her to focus
get her to look without using hocus pocus
won't blow this, seems hopeless
extremes poets must use to pole fish
feelin' her so much literally
sexual harassment, no I'm a wordsmith
gotta abort the plan to use Feelin' on ya Bootie to
flirt with
the V neck shirt fit
was thinking old school
but that's refurbished
so I repurpose my work wit
game affiliated type verses
worship her flows versus
nurses outfits that fit her perfect
oh shit, I mean ish
didn't mean to spit curses
or talk about my fantasies
with her and me, curses
what's worse is, I know I
need to get this thing right
if X airs before Y this mornin'
then we follows I, she probably catch that at nite
she takes flight, I know a site
she way whoa, I say might
when I cite, causes she likes
all these lines that I write
bite off more than I can chew

-Pikachu-
slow it down for yellow lights
but my confidence on 100
no elements cause my blight
she don't peep me now
handing her these bifocals to help her sight
equipped with infrared so
my heat she peeks at night
save some for a second date, just in case
I make it to first base tonight
my art similar to martial
if she tip-toes, we eye to eye
the same height
and, if she gets close to my face
I'm stealing kisses, poetic drama
cause I playwright.

Senses

I want to taste your tattoos
move smooth through
body moves
inhale your hair follicles too
then do what lovers do
fuse til we become the others muse
peruse curves that lead to
places I chose to lose
through you
found in grey hues and cues
that appear due
miss clues, like see through
look twice, peek-a-boo
from beau, you ask who
I say right, you say truuue
and…
I just want to
taste your tattoos.

\

in sync

I could hear it raining
and I guess the Earth needed to
respond like I did
when my soul finally admitted
you left because
you love yourself too.

These Days

These days I cry often
not because I'm weak
but because I stop hating
and found joy in tears
for reaching promises
kept long ago
and to those who remembered
reminding me that
these days are filled with love
invested now manifesting
in a gift I live daily
called the present.

Found and Lost

Anything lost
will be replaced by something better
so imagine how I felt
when I found
Me.

A Bit of Glamour

I told her she looked great naturally
and her response was
yeah, but sometimes
I like to add a bit of glamour
which I found to be
a quite satisfying reply.

See Through

I see you
past the make up
scares that's been laced up,
with broken promises.
I see you
hiding behind lies
posting pics with bright eyes
yet, what's behind those
windows to your soul
-nobody knows-
except those that take hold
to the love you think is cold,
wondering now
how I got here
warming myself up inside a heart
you locked
yeah,
you can't stop what is destiny.
I see you
at night, daily
in spirit and maybe
just maybe
you feel it, it's awakening
you think you're alone
in bed waiting,
underneath the sheets
with no illusions
I rode the wave at length
to soothe you.
I-see-you

with a taste like forbidden honey
but you gotta stop the running
I can show you something
turn the light on to escape the nothing,
I see you.

DM Sliding

Vision is steep
you I'm starting to peep
appearing to geek, while being a geek
digitally I speak
message discreate
see, I'm trying to meet over tea next week
directly, not needing to creep
your interest I'm scribing to see if I peek
play my uncustomary sonnet
consistently on repeat
seize your mind, intensity on a mil
smooth enough to put you to sleep
so subconsciously you can find me now
in the place that I was trying to reach.

Virtual Flirt

(Verse 1)

She asked me who am I
I'm askin' who are you
just might be a follower
that's leading from the booth
the truth of the matter
is the cosmos got me checking you
if everyone is shooting shots
I might as well just take a few
I knew what already happen
they call it déjà vu
baking chocolate chip type verses
peep One Poetic coming through
the view up here is lovely
come appreciate the hue
don't shoo me cause I'm too fly
give me props because they due
I suppose I'm over confident
oh well, let me show you who
exactly who I am, don't give a damn
what anyone thinks
and before I end this verse
I saw you smirk
as virtually at you I winked.

Let This Be

Sending this vibe through wind currents
felt on your butterfly wings
laying relaxed in water, bathed
sub conscious-ing ways
to have you feel this gaze
this pace
that keeps ramping up with every moment cased
pocketed in digitized pixels
staring relentlessly at energy
causing me to release
control, get a hold
of a meet and greet with your soul
healed from this cold
these freezer burns
that sought to scar my spirit
but missed
I hope you get
this, poet on fire
that's moving low
but flying higher than the light year
sitting three hundred and thirty-three galaxies
away, pass that synergy continually
from you to me
let this, Be.

That Kind of Love
(I found you through your eyes)

I need the love energy you had
as a teenager
with no restraint
or limits
relentless,
pure.

Listening to Her

While meditating
to a melody
in-between euphony
I found myself focusing
on HER
as she,
sang in key
to God
directly
to me.

What She Said...

She said she loved my poetry
and maybe she doesn't realize
but,
to say that to me means,
you love me.

About Last Night

I made love with God
while slow songs played
and I laid some where between
cloud nine and the outer edge of orbit,
surprised how beautiful
the new moon looked
as I caressed
my unorthodox sonnets
from the inner depth
of my solar plexus
surged past surface level
and met Her at the tip
of conception,
as our souls found love unconditioned in
memories wrapped right
in intimate pain,
if energy had breath
you'd see it during this winter night
between this moment of heat
and the first kiss we shared
in the sunset and,
I-should-have-took-a-picture
framed it in eternity
so I could forget how love felt daily
erasing the algorithm
and relieve the experience
after every known and unknown form
of punctuation.

I Heard Too

She only told the moon
but didn't know I was listenin'
it wasn't my intention
but it happened while I was wishin'
upon a star, from afar
she didn't know who I are
door left ajar, laid I par
heard the secret bar for bar
pennies for my thoughts now and
she might have to go get the coin jar
cause the moon wasn't the only one listen'
but your secret we both won't mar.

2 Inches Between

It felt good to feel your embrace
after months of just seeing your face
and I wanted to take that moment
extend it so I can feel my cheek pressed
to your stomach, clutch
like 3 seconds left on the clock
feels right so I'll take the shot
not a vaccine, more like
by a flying object landing between
the spot with no X to mark targets
I've long since listened to intuition
that mentioned a blue-eyed bandit
lurking ever so close,
finding you behind screen doors
I bypass as if no glass came between us
now, that you're here
the here and now is that much better
put it in a lyric
charge it with a bit of lust and playful
mix it with trust and caring
and what you're staring at is love letters
formed to make words from the alphabet soup
taste like sweet, feels like butterflies
released from my stomach
that's where feelings for you reside
and I…think I…might just have fallen
for you.

For a Moment

She was my lyric
dancing to her own rhythm
singing songs through fingertips
clutching sticks
that etched artistic reality
I desired to capture the moment
but caged birds don't sing
like free ones
so here's to me watching
you tiptoe through lullabies
kissing canvases with particles
made of stars and moons
and as you shine
my eyes reflect the beauty there within
of this moment of balance and love.

Heavenly Abode

Cosmic cable
tuned in on
channel two twenty-two
and you,
you're on ultraviolet spectrums
for everyone to see within
envisioned luminously
transposed from thought
to meditation
integrated between
stardust and love
one and the same
but couldn't be more different
hatch the idea that
the limits of senses
doesn't stop the endearment in this sentence
from being presented
metaphorically on your cheek
keep that same energy
found on infinite
so when the atom splits
we'll remember this moment
forever.

Moon Lotus

I can feel your smile
and laugh
taste those lips
your essence
sense your glow
the radiance
I think I
need a cycle of it
sunflower, I'm noticing
the attraction pull
I envision this
like molecules meeting
soft hands reaching
peace seeking in eyes
fingers in curls of hair
I'm taking the dare
of pressing my lips
into yours
-not onto but into-
to merge shadows in light
to crest bright with night
and this might
be the garden that Eden
was made for
loc us in
as frame rates from photos
that establish the pause
for a moment
as your arms raised

sweet like honey
and I'm daydreaming of
inner visions that breathe
like leaves, like petals
this is life
through your skin.

Metaspiritual Energy

I feel like, I could
place my fingertips on your face
replace the space between with our lips
holding this moment
as close as your breath to my skin
press that loop button
feel this on repeat
scratched the surface and already in too deep
upgrade this from physical pleasantries
to unconditional math
sew back the cloth we were cut from
deposit dark into your light molecules for balance
find your essence in nearby verses
so every version receives this love
this step now beyond next level
that's found and lost through eons
the flame that mirrors time
at 11:11.

Heaven on Earth
(Twin Flame 11:11)

The polarity - contradiction
finished at the beginning
our love is both and unconfined
I finally realized what we are doing
broken from shackles
the need to unlearn, reprogram
then make like fire in rain
the world can keep fixed styles
just so, freed verses explain
the accepted duality
I live in your dreams
on shifted time lines that redefined
many of the things I was lead to believe
accepting me for me
was the gateway to all of you
it's no wonder
time alone was more of us
learning each other from
the inside out
never too late
caught in just the nick of this lifetime
let's enjoy our forever
together in ways that now
the universe couldn't separate.

That Just Happened

What happens when
you recognize I love you,
does the time spent sitting
feeling "it" in my stomach
unable to focus on much else
make a difference,
as I too get myself together
put on this façade that you see right through
that which, no, whom this
experience I'm experimenting with
is pleasant enough
it's my soul that wishes
the human side of me could touch
current manifestations that now exist
in front of me
merge this desire with the passion created
for the situation at hand
come interlock your fingers into mine
and inhale deep these words
that cycle through your every molecule
admitting I fill you up
move this thought of "what are we"
out the box we started in
and enjoy the rain just as much as the sunshine
as long as it's done jointly, to the point
you stop mid sentence amongst friends
recognizing, I'm inside you
and I'm inclined to end this

with images of beautiful
not limited to words but
found sitting pretty
and, oh so lovely
in your eyes.

The Toast

It's been said
that we should make this love forever
however, this love we have
has transcended the stretch of the word existence
found each other on Earth for this encore
as the allure of our magic at its core
is another tale or lore to add to our collection
the blessing of this verse is
that at our worst, the best will have to come
some may find it authentic
but this, this is original
the only of its kind
you and I are stardust in the heavens
a breath of fresh air
we're tears that stream from happiness
there's no need to compare
combined at the hip, heart and lips
it's like when the sun met the moon
and sealed it with a kiss
this light, this world of love personified
got dissected but then we realized
that at our core, the Universe resides
so no matter what goes on, on the outside
inside we'll always have each other
that's, one another
that's, two lovers uncovered
ready for what it is to discover
in this lifetime of shine
now that two are now realigned
as one heart, one soul and
one mind.

Alter

I'm in love with you
without ever meeting you
or learning who you are
from building a physical relationship,
I care "less" for the societal belief
that says different about
my soul proclamation,
synchronization speaks different
and it's only my human existence
that lingers in wonder
that my mind wishes to defer to but
I love you,
I choose this
shifted destiny to escape
continuous loops
sitting for hours on end
manifesting, absent of mind
so you can feel me clear
mirror the moon for light
connect in alignment
there is no wrong or right
just decisions made
real, authentic
linked to reasons only stood
under, over and thoroughly in-between,
so here's what I mean
when I say I love you
and - only you can decide
what's next.

Transmission in Progress

Sending this through a water hole
so you can hear this clearly
no need for currency
as previous advancements cover
the loan of souls in this lifetime,
pulsate power from heartbeats
had to wait for planets to line up
to figure a way to ask
what's all this mean,
pushing boundaries so you can
find my trail, hear these echoes
as Mother Nature meets Father Time
co-signs of the same signs
we are shadows in space
that escaped the matrix
and what were faced with
is a language that speaks binary,
but to the contrary, this is verse
between bi and everything
in an infinite spectrum,
transmission started
now, standing by
to be received.

About The Author

Billy Williams, Jr. was born to write poetry. Poetically knows as B-Dot and OnePoeticGamer, the life as a poet all started because of a girl back in 7th grade. Seeing he had a gift with words, he began to use his energy to produce poetry that spoke to various genres.

Hailing from Raleigh, North Carolina, Billy is a poet, educator, coach, gamer, streamer and motivator. The I prelude I is Billy's second book of published poetry, with more poetry books to be released in the near future.

If you want to find out more information about Billy's upcoming books, you can contact him by way of e-mail at onepoeticgamer@amazulugaming.com or sending a message to him from the following website www.amazulugaming.com. If you wish to know more about his gaming/streaming life, check him at www.twitch.tv/onepoeticgamer.

Social Media Contacts

Poetry Blog: www.amazulugaming.com
Instagram: Onepoeticgamer
Twitch: www.twitch.tv/onepoeticgamer

AmaZulu Gaming, LLC

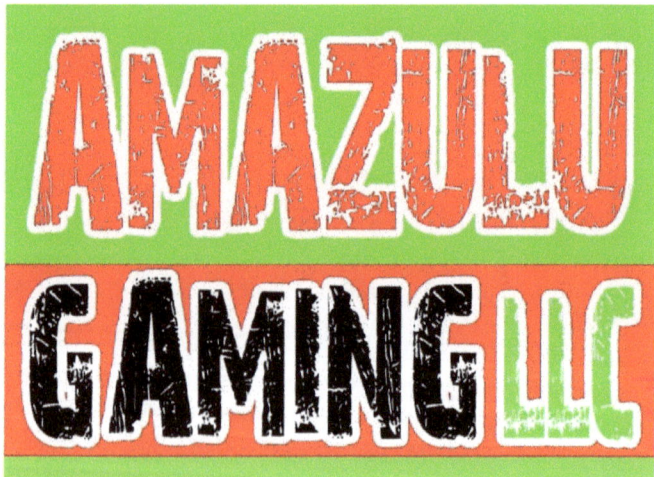

Poetry Books Written By One Poetic

Poetic Superhero

Everybody is looking for a hero. Poetic Superhero is here for you.

The I prElude I

In order to find we, HE must find himself before finding SHE.

His Emotions Released

This is written for Her…I'm glad I finally got Her attention.

School Dad

Poetry inspired by 16 years of working as an educator in elementary, middle and high school.

the Book of HER

33 poems for HER.

Poetic Flows - A Book of Rhymes (upcoming soon)

When I feel the flow, I let go with words.

Excommunicated (A Bard's Tale)
(upcoming soon)

Exit wounds given by another can lead to one's salvation.

Leftover Love Poems (Future Release)

Sometimes you'll get things humanely wrong just so your soul can get right.

HER - The Collection (Poetry Anthology)
(Future Release)

Includes works from The I pr.E.lude I, His Emotions Released and the Book of HER.

Spoken Word By One Poetic

Blue Room Mix Tape
(upcoming soon)